Comptroller of the Currency
Administrator of National Banks

Real Estate Loans

Comptroller's Handbook
(Section 213)

Narrative - March 1990, Procedures - March 1998

A

Assets

Real Estate Loans
(Section 213)

Table of Contents

Real Estate Loans
(Section 213)   Introduction

Any national banking association may make real estate loans, subject to the law set forth at 12 USC 371 and 12 CFR 34. Those loans generally can be defined as loans primarily secured by real property. However, the law does recognize different types of real estate loans.

Real Estate Loan Policy

The bank must also establish a policy that determines:

- The maximum amount that may be loaned on a given loan.
- The maximum aggregate amount that may be loaned in a given category.
- The maximum aggregate amount that may be loaned on all real estate loans.
- The need for amortization on certain loans and the amount of annual amortization required.

The degree of risk inherent in a real estate loan depends on the loan amount, the interest rate, and other special terms. A consideration of the value of the real property over the anticipated life of the loan is of major importance.

The bank's policies and procedures should include an appraisal program. Appraisals are professional judgments of the present and/or future value of the real property. The following are the general approaches used to determine value:

- Cost Approach — In this approach, the replacement cost of the building and improvements is estimated, estimated depreciation is deducted, and the value of the site is added. The reliability of such a valuation depends on an appraiser's skill. As the property increases in age, both replacement cost and depreciation become more difficult to estimate.

- Market Data or Direct Sales Comparison Approach — The essence of this approach is to determine the price that similar properties have sold for recently on the local market and, through an appropriate adjustment process, to estimate the fair market value of the subject property based on these comparable sales. In general, when adequate sales data are available, an appraiser will give the most weight to this type of estimate, however, often the available market data is not sufficient to justify a conclusion. As comparability (in terms of property characteristics, market, financing, terms, or timing) of sales data decreases, the reliability of estimates based on such factors also decreases.

- Capitalization of Income Approach — In this approach, the net income a property is expected to produce over time is converted into an estimate of its present value. The accuracy of this method depends on the appraiser's skill in estimating the anticipated future net income of the property and in selecting the appropriate capitalization rate and method.

- Discounted Cash Flow Approach — In this approach a discount rate is applied to variable, positive or negative net income streams to reflect their present value. The sale of the property at the end of its holding period is also discounted and added to the overall valuation. Like the previous approach, the accuracy of this method is dependent on the appraiser's ability to arrive at a discount rate, estimate future income streams for the property, and determine a reasonable sales price at the end of the holding period.

Bank management should ensure that appraisers are adequately qualified and independent. The appraiser's background should be reviewed to ensure he has received adequate training and has had experience with the type of property being appraised. Also, the appraiser should not be involved with the lending or collection functions of the bank, nor have a financial or other interest in the property. Appraiser's reports should be in written form, include a reasonable valuation method for determining market value, and contain support for all assumptions and projections used in arriving at the real estate's value.

Procedures should be established to ensure all newly received appraisals are reviewed for reasonableness and for ordering new appraisals where needed. New appraisals may be needed for several reasons including deteriorating economic conditions, changes in the borrower's financial capacity, or when renewals or extensions of the loan are being considered. They might also be used as an audit procedure to identify overvaluation of collateral or unsatisfactory appraisers.

The appraisal report is only one factor to consider when granting real estate loans. Many banks have incurred significant loan losses and large amounts of other real estate owned for placing too much or sole reliance on the appraisal. The bank's real estate loan policy should ensure that loans are granted with the reasonable probability that the debtor will be able and willing to meet the payment terms. Any loan that does not meet that standard should be regarded as unsound, regardless of the collateral value and favorable ratio of collateral value to the outstanding loan.

Environmental Risk

Lenders should ensure that real estate offered as collateral is not affected by the presence of hazardous materials. High levels of asbestos in commercial buildings, chemically contaminated soil, and underground water supplies, or use of the property for the production or storage of toxic materials are but a few of the sources of environmental risk which may subject the bank to potential liability. Preferably, such risks should be identified prior to funding a loan or offering any type of commitment to lend. However, where the bank discovers that it has already accepted contaminated property as collateral, it should take steps to monitor the situation so as to minimize any potential liability on the part of the bank.

Where the bank has reason to believe that there may be serious environmental problems associated with property that it holds as collateral, it should seek the advice and assistance of individuals with expertise in dealing with environmental risk. The need for expert advice becomes especially critical if the bank finds itself in the position of having to decide whether to foreclose on a contaminated property. Although, federal laws dealing with the control and clean-up of hazardous waste contain "innocent landowner defenses" which offer banks some protection, those defenses can easily be lost if certain conditions not met.

Unsound Mortgage Loans

A first mortgage loan generally is unsound if:

- Its liquidation depends on the sale of the underlying real estate.
- The amount of the loan is large relative to the fair value of the property.
- The ability of the obligor to pay is questionable.
- The loan has remained dormant a long time, indicating that its transfer to

another obligor through the sale of the realty will become necessary.

Other elements such as interest and tax arrearages can be significant, but they are generally corollaries of the situations outlined above.

A principal indication of an unsound real estate loan is an improper relationship between the amount of the loan, the potential sale price of the property, and the availability of a market. The potential sale price of a property may or may not be the same as its appraised value. In dealing with unsound mortgage loans, the current potential sale price or liquidating value of the realty is of primary importance, and the appraised value is of secondary importance. There may be little or no current demand for the property at its appraised value, and it may have to be disposed of at a sacrifice value.

A mortgage loan should be considered "potential other real estate" when the examiner is reasonably convinced that it will have to be liquidated by a sale of the realty and when no reasonably tangible and definite arrangements for that sale have been made.

The term "mortgagee in possession" refers to one who has lawfully acquired possession of mortgaged premises to enforce the security on such property. When a mortgagee receives the rents or other profits generated by the property, it is not a mortgagee in possession unless control of the real estate is removed from the hands of the mortgagor. Generally, a bank may be considered as mortgagee in possession if it is collecting the rents or operating the mortgaged property and has ceased to look to the mortgagor for payment of the loan.

Mortgaged premises can be considered foreclosed, in substance, regardless of whether formal foreclosure has taken place. Statement of Financial Accounting Standards No. 15 requires that foreclosure accounting be applied to collateral when the debtor has little to no equity in the collateral, sources of repayment depend on the operation or sale of the collateral, and the debtor has abandoned control of the collateral. In some cases, the debtor might still retain control of the collateral, but because of financial weakness or economic prospects, it is unlikely the debtor will be able to rebuild equity in the collateral.

Real estate loans which meet the criteria for a substantive foreclosure or in which the bank is mortgagee in possession, should be considered "other real estate." For additional considerations relating to such assets, see the section

"Other Real Estate Owned."

Historically, many banks have jeopardized their capital structures by granting ill-considered real estate mortgage loans. Apart from unusual, localized, adverse economic conditions that could not have been foreseen resulting in a temporary or permanent "wash out" of realty values, the principal errors made in granting real estate loans have included:

- Inadequate regard to normal realty values during periods when it is in great demand, thus inflating the price structure.
- Inadequate regard to mortgage loan amortization.
- Inadequate regard to the maximum debt load and paying capacity of the borrower.
- Failure to reasonably restrict mortgage loans on properties for which there is limited demand.

Examiners must appraise, not only individual mortgage loans, but also the overall mortgage lending and administration policies of the bank to ascertain the relative soundness of its mortgage loan operations.

Home Equity Lines of Credit

Home equity lines of credit (HELCs), although not new to some bank's real estate lending activities, have become increasingly popular in recent years. HELCs are primarily open-ended credit facilities secured by a lien against the equity in residential property. HELCs offer variable rates, flexible repayment terms and can be accessed by check, cash advance, credit card, telephone transfer, or through ATMs. Additional characteristics of this product include relatively low interest rates as opposed to other forms of consumer credit, absorption by some banks of certain fees (origination, title search, property appraisal, recordation, etc.) generally associated with opening a real estate mortgage, and changes imposed by the Tax Reform Act of 1986 regarding the deductibility of interest paid on consumer debt.

As with other forms of real estate lending, banks should adopt specific policies and procedures. Strategic plans should incorporate HELC processes fully. Management should have expertise in mortgage lending as well as open-end credit. A major concern is that borrowers will become overextended and the bank will have to initiate foreclosure proceedings. Therefore, underwriting standards should emphasize the borrower's ability to service the line from cash flow rather than the sale of collateral, especially if the HELCs are written on a variable rate basis. When the bank has offered a low introductory rate, repayment capacity should be analyzed at the rate that could be in effect at the conclusion of the initial term. Acceptable loan-to-value and debt-to-income ratios should be established. Proper credit and collateral documentation, including adequate appraisals and evidence of lien priority status, should be required. Another significant risk is the issue of continued lien priority. State laws dictate whether subsequent advances under a line of credit continue to hold lien priority status. Programs that include sufficient periodic reviews of the borrower's financial condition, particularly when the line has been inactive for some time and is nearing maturity, should be developed. Procedures for a "pre-maturity review" with the customer should be established to prevent a "crisis based" evaluation.

Coordination among banking departments is essential. Legal, consumer disclosure, and asset/liability management issues are present in HELCs. Proposed risk based capital requirements could also affect a bank offering a HELC program. Examiners should be aware of any violations discovered during the most recent consumer compliance examination and ensure that corrective action has been effected.

All examiners should be familiar with the various consumer credit laws and regulations and be alert to potential violations in this area during a supervisory presence. The Competitive Equality Banking Act of 1987 requires banks opening home equity accounts after December 9, 1987 to establish a life-of-plan interest rate ceiling on those accounts.

Appropriate systems should be established that provide accurate, detailed, and timely information regarding HELCs. Reports could address total commitments, outstandings, account activity, delinquencies, non-accruals, and extensions/renewals. Adequate software capable of calculating accurate disclosures and payments should be retained.

Adjustable-Rate Mortgages

Effective March 27, 1981, the Office of the Comptroller of the Currency (OCC) issued an adjustable-rate mortgage regulation to encourage national bank participation in the residential mortgage market. 12 CFR 29 facilitates the development of new mortgage instruments that are responsive to changing interest rates, deposit and liability structures, and borrower needs. The regulation establishes standards on the information that must be disclosed to prospective borrowers. Interest rate changes may be implemented through changes in the amount of the installment payment or the rate of amortization. Changing the rate of amortization affects the life of the loan and, moreover, introduces the potential for increases to the outstanding balance (negative amortization).

Comments or criticisms of real estate loans should be confined to the risk of a particular loan, policy decisions on the relationship of real estate loans to the bank's asset or deposit structure, legality of specific loans, adequacy of appraisal policies, and similar items. The most convincing proof of the quality and soundness of a real estate mortgage loan is a favorable payment history. Conversely, a long dormant real estate mortgage loan is never desirable, no matter how adequately protected by the value of the underlying realty. The regular payment history of real estate mortgage loans is essential to their continued soundness and desirability.

General Procedures

These procedures are intended to determine the adequacy of the bank's policies, procedures, and internal controls as they relate to residential, home equity lending, reverse mortgages and affordable housing programs. The extent of testing and procedures performed should be based upon the examiner's assessment of risk. This assessment should include consideration of work performed by other regulatory agencies, internal and external auditors, other internal compliance review units, formalized policies and procedures, and the effectiveness of internal controls and management information systems (MIS).

Objective: To set the scope for assessing the quantity of risk and quality of risk management in residential, home equity, reverse mortgages, and affordable housing lending.

1. Review the following documents to identify any previous problems that require follow-up. Determine if bank management satisfactorily responded to any adverse findings.

   ☐ Supervisory strategy in the OCC's Electronic Information System.
   ☐ EIC's scope memorandum.
   ☐ Previous Report of Examination.
   ☐ Working papers from the previous examination.
   ☐ Internal/external audit reports and working papers, if necessary.
   ☐ Correspondence memorandum.
   ☐ Loan review reports.

2. From the EIC, obtain the results of his/her analysis of the UBPR, BERT, or other OCC reports. Identify any concerns, trends, or changes in residential, home equity, reverse mortgages, and affordable housing lending.

3. In addition to general information requested in LPM, obtain and review other internal reports management uses to supervise residential, home equity, reverse mortgages, and affordable housing lending. Some examples include:

   ☐ The budget at the beginning of the year, and budget revisions as of the examination date.
   ☐ An organization chart including each functional area.

☐ Copies of formal job descriptions for all principal department positions.

☐ Resumes of principals in the department.

☐ Copies of management compensation programs, including incentive plans.

☐ Copies of any board reports concerning residential, home equity, reverse mortgages, and affordable housing lending operations since the last examination.

☐ Copies of key management reports used by department management.

☐ Copies of all internal and external audit reports and loan review reports covering residential, home equity, reverse mortgages, and affordable housing lending since the last examination, and copies of any management responses.

☐ Descriptions of all codes and abbreviations used on computer-generated reports.

☐ A list of board and executive or senior management committees that supervise residential, home equity, reverse mortgages, and affordable housing lending, including a list of members and meeting schedules. Also obtain copies of minutes documenting those meetings since the last examination.

☐ A summary listing of all residential, home equity, reverse mortgage, and affordable housing loan products offered and a brief description of their characteristics, including pricing.

☐ Copies of marketing plans for the residential, home equity, reverse mortgage, and affordable housing lending department overall and by product.

☐ Copies of loan policies and procedures for all residential, home equity, reverse mortgage, and affordable housing lending products.

☐ A list of scoring systems in use and copies of their manuals. Also obtain a list of credit bureaus used as well as a description of any credit bureau scoring that is used.

☐ A list of residential, home equity, reverse mortgage, or affordable housing securitizations and copies of the prospectus' associated with those offerings.

☐ A balance sheet and income and expense statement as of the examination date and most recent year-end.

☐ Residential, home equity, reverse mortgage and affordable housing delinquencies.

4. Obtain loan MIS reports, as needed:

☐ Summary reports showing trends in outstandings, new volume, delinquencies, new loan and portfolio yield by different product types (e.g., residential, home equity, reverse mortgage, affordable housing), etc.

☐ Credit scoring distribution reports by portfolio, new volume, delinquencies, and losses.

☐ Residential, home equity, reverse mortgages, affordable housing past-due reports, nonaccrual list, and trial balance.

☐ Extension and renewal reports for the latest month-end and previous month-end summaries.

5.   Obtain the following from either the LPM examiner or the bank EIC:

☐ Any useful information obtained from the review of minutes of the loan and discount committee or any similar committee.
☐ Reports related to residential, home equity, reverse mortgage, and affordable housing lending that have been furnished to the loan and discount committee (or similar committee), or the board of directors.
☐ List of directors, executive officers, principal shareholders, and their interests.

6.   Verify the completeness of requested information with the request list.

7.   Review internal bank reports on the residential, home equity, reverse mortgage, and affordable housing lending department. Determine any material changes in the following:

- Types of products offered.
- Volume of business.
- Changes in market focus.
- Levels and trends in delinquencies.

8.   Determine, during early discussions with management:

- Any significant changes in policies, practices, or personnel relating to activities, systems, loan approval, or collection processes.
- Material changes in products, volumes, and changes in market focus.
- Levels and trends in delinquencies for each loan type.
- Any internal or external factors that could affect residential, home equity, reverse mortgage, and affordable housing lending operations.

9.   Based on the performance of these steps and discussions with the bank EIC, determine the scope of this examination and its objectives.

Note: Select steps necessary to meet objectives from among the following examination procedures. All steps are seldom required in an examination.

Note: As procedures are performed, determine whether bank officers are operating in conformance with established guidelines.

Quantity of Risk

Conclusion: The quantity of risk is (low, moderate, high).

Objectives: To determine the quantity of risk relative to residential and home equity lending including an evaluation of the portfolio for credit quality and collectability.

1.   Evaluate the reasonableness of management's business and strategic plans for the department. Consider the following:

   - Are they clear?
   - Do they reflect the department's current direction?
   - Are they consistent with overall bank objectives?

Department Performance

1.   Evaluate the residential, home equity, reverse mortgage, and affordable housing lending department's performance by conducting the following:

   - Compare actual performance to budget.
   - By using management reports and the UBPR, review management's and the department's performance by analyzing:
     - Profitability trends.
     - Delinquency trends.
     - Loss and recovery trends.
   - Discuss adverse trends and large or unusual variances to budget with management.

Marketing

1.   Evaluate the risk in the bank's marketing plans by:

   - Assessing the appropriateness of the data used to develop the plans.
   - Ascertaining whether any market, economic, or profitability studies were done either externally or internally.
   - Determining whether risks (credit, transaction, liquidity, interest rate, compliance, strategic, and reputation) are sufficiently addressed in the plans.
   - Determining whether plans incorporate a loosening or tightening of credit standards.
   - Determining whether plans appropriately address the stated direction and goals of the residential and home equity lending department and the bank, as

---

a whole.

2. Assess the level of credit risk for all new residential, home equity, reverse mortgage, and affordable housing products implemented since the last examination and, to the extent possible, those planned products. Consider:

- Reasonableness of underwriting guidelines.
- Performance of products.
- Volume and significance of underwriting exception levels.

3. Assess the risks associated with different home equity solicitation methods, (e.g., preapproved loans versus individual loan applications). Consider:

- Selection criteria for pre-approvals.
- Response rate to solicitations.
- Performance of accounts compared to marketing projections/goals.

4. If used, ensure that prescreening complies with applicable consumer legislation, particularly anti-discrimination laws and regulations (refer to Banking Bulletin 91-50).

Underwriting

1. Evaluate the quantity of risk in the portfolio as the testing procedures are performed.

2. Determine, for liquidity purposes, if the bank follows the Fannie Mae and Freddie Mac underwriting guidelines for extending residential mortgages. (This would ensure access to the secondary market if funding is needed.)

Testing

For residential and home equity lending, there are detailed testing procedures for six areas; underwriting practices, score overrides, loan renewals and extensions, MIS, FHA and VA insured/guaranteed loans, and loan participations purchased or sold. Prior to performing any testing procedures, you will need to determine which areas require thorough examination. All tests do not necessarily need to be performed at each examination. Deciding which tests are needed depends on the individual bank's risk profile and the scope of their residential and home equity lending activities.

1.	Identify which tests need to be performed. Consider the following:

- The risk profile of the bank to include the following:
    – Areas of risk identified during the last examination.
    – Areas of risk identified during the performance of the general procedures.
    – The scope of the bank's residential, home equity, reverse mortgage, and affordable housing lending activities.
    – The types of products offered, especially new products or significant increases in existing products.
- Areas of risk identified by the Loan Review and Audit functions.
- Input from the bank EIC.

2.	Perform the procedures for the following areas based on the areas of risk identified.

Underwriting practices:

1.	Select a sample of new loans booked in the past 30-180 days from a current trial balance, using a numerical statistical sampling technique. (The audit department may be able to help select a sample using their software.)

2.	Set up a worksheet to include the following testing criteria:

- Policy guidelines.
- Underwriting terms.
- Collateral documentation requirements.
- Pricing information.

3.	Conduct the file review by transcribing the worksheet information from credit files, automated systems, and/or MIS reports.

4.	During your sample review, evaluate the quality of underwriting practices by determining the following:

- Compliance with policy guidelines, including credit criteria, documentation, pricing, terms, etc.
- The credit quality of new loans and whether the quality has changed since the last examination.
- The volume (number and size) and significance of approved policy exceptions.
- Level of classified/criticized loans.

Score Model Overrides:

1. Pull a sample of new loans booked in the last 30-90 days, that scored below the "cutoff" but were approved anyway, as follows:

    *   Select loans using a numerical statistical sampling technique. The audit department may be able to help select a sample using their software.
    *   For selecting sample loans, use reports related to the test.

2. Set up a worksheet to include the following testing criteria:

    *   Policy override guidelines.
    *   Reason(s) for the override.
    *   Appropriateness of the credit decision.

3. Conduct the file review by transcribing the worksheet information from credit files and/or other applicable reports.

4. During the sample review, determine:

    *   Compliance with override policy requirements.
    *   The appropriateness of the credit decision.

Loan renewals and extensions:

1. Pull a sample of loans as follows:

    *   From the entire population to test usage and accuracy of reporting.
    *   From the renewal and extension listing to test compliance with policy.

2. Set up a worksheet to include the following criteria:

    *   Loan renewal and extension policy guidelines.
    *   Number of extension(s)/renewal(s)
    *   Justification or support for the decision(s).
    *   Accuracy of reported information.

3. Conduct the file review by transcribing the worksheet information from credit files and/or other applicable reports.

4. During the sample review, determine:

    *   Compliance with renewal/extension policy requirements.

- The degree of usage.
- The appropriateness of the decision.
- The accuracy of the reported information.

MIS:

1. During the various testing procedures, verify the accuracy of MIS by:

   - Tracing reportable items to appropriate listings/reports including past dues, renewal and extensions, prepayments, and insider loans.

FHA insured loans and VA guaranteed loans:

1. Pull a sample of loans from the entire population.

2. Test each sample loan to determine that:

   - Each loan has a valid certificate of insurance or guaranty.
   - Each loan is recorded on past due listings and/or delinquency reports submitted to government agencies.

Loans and Participations Purchased and Sold:

1. If the bank purchases residential or home equity lines, pull a sample of recent loans from that population.

2. Test each sample loan to determine that adequate credit standards have been implemented to ensure proper credit evaluation.

3. Review participation certificates and records to ascertain that the parties share in the risks and contractual payments on a pro rata basis.

4. Investigate any participations sold immediately prior to the examination to determine if they were sold to avoid possible criticism during this examination.

Testing Summary:

1. For all testing performed, consolidate exceptions and any unusual patterns.

Collections

1. Using key collection reports used by management, review collection activity, noting any changing conditions and adverse trends.

2. Assess the adequacy of information in key collection reports used by

management.

3. Review renewal, extension, overlimit, and deferral programs. Determine the extent used and the appropriateness of the volume.

4. Review loan debit and credit suspense items by:

- Identifying any large or stale items.
- Discussing with management and charging-off the old items as appropriate.

5. Evaluate the listings of delinquent loans and foreclosed property and determine if write-downs and charge-offs comply with bank policy.

6. If loans and foreclosures have not been written down or charged-off in line with policy guidelines:

- Prepare a listing of exceptions.
- Discuss the accounts with management.

7. Classify any delinquent loans and foreclosed property, as appropriate.

8. Review any reports on delinquent and defaulted government agency guaranteed loans and determine if:

- Management is accurately informed.
- Management is complying with the reporting requirements.
- Claims are being promptly filed after default.

Securitization

1. Review reports detailing each outstanding asset securitization and any in process.

2. Review the securitization agreements and determine:

- The significant terms of each securitization.
- Any practices which may create liability or recourse for the bank.

3. Evaluate the performance of each securitization by:

- Comparing performance to terms of the securitization.

- Discussing significant performance trends with management.

4. Determine if the bank routinely repurchases past due loans from the securitization. If there is a pattern of repurchases, investigate the recourse implications on the accounting treatment (i.e., whether the securitization is accounted for as a financing or sale).

5. Evaluate the impact of collection programs, such as extensions, on performance reports to investors.

6 Review the accounting treatment for securitizations, and determine how the bank established its accounting treatment.

6. If concerns are identified, refer to the "Asset Securitization" handbook for additional examination procedures.

Concentrations of Credit

1. Coordinate with the examiner responsible for "Concentrations of Credit" to ensure applicable procedures are performed.

Allowance for Loan and Lease Losses

1. Assess the adequacy of the ALLL provision for residential, home equity, reverse mortgages, and affordable housing loans by using the most recent quarter-end analysis. Consider:

   - Whether management's analysis is documented.
   - If the analysis properly recognizes the risks in the portfolio.

2. Forward the results of your analysis to the ALLL examiner.

Compliance with Laws and Regulations

Objective: Determine the level of compliance with laws, regulations and rulings pertaining to residential, home equity, reverse mortgage, and affordable housing lending.

1. Test compliance with the following laws, rulings, and regulations:

   - *12 USC 84 and 12 CFR 32—Legal Lending Limits.*
   - *12 USC 375a, 12 CFR 215, and 12 USC 375b—Loans to Insiders.*
   - *12 CFR 2—Disposition of Credit Life Insurance Income.*
   - *12 CFR 371c—Loans to Affiliates.*

- *18 USC 215—Commission or Gift for Procuring Loan.*
- *2 USC 431(8)(B) and 2 USC 441b—Political Contributions and Loans.*
- *12 USC 1972—Tie-in Provisions.*
- *12 USC 371 and 12 CFR 34—Real Estate Loans.*
- *12 CFR 34 Subpart B—Adjustable-Rate Mortgages.*

2. Determine if the consumer compliance examination uncovered any violations and whether corrective action was taken.

3. If significant violations or exceptions are found, expand the test to:

- Evaluate subsequent compliance with any law or regulation.
- Determine that previously identified problems have been corrected.

Verification Procedures

Objective: Verify the bank's residential, home equity, reverse mortgage, and affordable housing loans, and test the accuracy of the bank's records and adequacy of record keeping.

1. Test footings to the trial balance.

2. If verification procedures are considered necessary, use an appropriate sampling technique to select loans from the trial balance or use loans previously selected.

3. For sample loans to be verified, do the following:

- Ensure the books and records properly reflect the bank's liability.
- Check calculations of service and interest charges included in the last billing.
- Check debt instruments for completeness and agree date, amount, and terms to the trial balance.
- Verify that the approving officer has approved the note.
- Compare collateral documentation in the files with the description on the collateral register.
- List and investigate any collateral discrepancies.
- Determine that any required insurance coverage is adequate and the bank is named as loss payee.
- Ensure that each home equity line is evidenced by a properly completed loan agreement.

4. If the bank charges fees for residential, home equity, reverse mortgage, and affordable housing lending services, perform the following procedures:

- Using accounts selected from the sample selected in procedure two above, check the computation of the charges and reasonableness of assessed fees.
- Trace charges to posting in the appropriate general ledger income account.
- Review monthly income amounts posted to the general ledger for reasonableness compared to the number of accounts handled.

5. Scan accrued interest and income accounts for any unusual entries and follow up on any unusual items by tracing to initial and supporting records.

6. Obtain or prepare a schedule showing the amount of monthly interest income and home equity balances since the last examination and:

    - Calculate or check yield.
    - Investigate any significant fluctuations or trends.

7. Using a list on non-accruing loans/lines, check accrual records to determine that interest income is not being recorded.

8. For all applicable loans:

    - Review escrow agreement provisions for real estate taxes and/or insurance and determine if undisbursed amounts are at least equal to the provisions of the agreement.
    - If escrow accounts are maintained for real estate taxes and/or insurance, determine if debit entries to those accounts are authorized in accordance with the terms of the loan agreement and if they are supported by individual bills or other evidence.

Quality of Risk Management

Conclusion: The quality of risk management is (strong, satisfactory, weak).

Policy

Conclusion: The board (has/has not) established effective policies and standards governing residential, home equity, reverse mortgages, and affordable housing lending.

Objective: To determine if the board of directors has adopted policies and underwriting standards that are consistent with safe and sound banking practices and appropriate to the size of the bank and the nature and scope of its operations.

1. Determine if the board of directors, consistent with its duties and responsibilities, has adopted a written residential, home equity, reverse mortgages, and affordable housing loan policy. The policy should address the following:

   - Marketing.
   - Underwriting.
   - Portfolio administration.
   - Collection.
   - Foreclosure.
   - Write-downs or charge-offs.

2. Determine that the board reviews and approves of the policy annually.

3. Determine, during the board's review, that they evaluate the existing policy to determine if it complies with changing market conditions.

4. Review the bank's underwriting standards as outlined in the board-approved policy and evaluate:

   - The adequacy and reasonableness of underwriting guidelines.
   - The recognition of risks, including credit, transaction, and compliance risks.
   - The sufficiency of guidelines provided (for example, ensure that parameters for the acceptance or rejection of risk are well-delineated).
   - Whether credit limits on loans and loan officer approvals are reasonable.
   - The adequacy of renewal and extension guidelines.
   - The written system to ensure compliance with policy standards.

---

5. Review the adequacy of the renewal, extension, restructure, overlimit, and deferral program policies.

6. If the bank engages in asset securitization, review and evaluate the bank's asset securitization policy by:

   - Discussing with management the collection policies applied to the securitized portfolio.
   - Reviewing bank established risk limits on recourse for bad paper.

Processes

Conclusion: Management and the board (have/have not) established effective processes relating to residential, home equity, reverse mortgage, and affordable housing lending.

Objective: To determine if processes, including internal controls, are adequate and consistent with prudent underwriting practices.

Management

1. Evaluate management's process for periodically reviewing and/or revising policies and procedures. Consider:

   - Whether the process effectively incorporates necessary and timely changes.
   - Whether controls are adequate to ensure a review by all necessary parties prior to adoption.

2. Determine the method used to communicate policies and procedures to staff. Through discussions with staff members, evaluate the effectiveness and timeliness of the communication system.

3. Assess the process management uses to identify and monitor exceptions to policy.

Marketing

1. Evaluate management's process for developing and implementing marketing plans, noting time frames for activities and the approval process (i.e., who approves and when).

2. Evaluate the adequacy of management tools used to monitor the performance of marketing plans.

3.   Discuss the new product development process with management and assess its adequacy. Specifically determine and evaluate the following:

- That appropriate feasibility studies are performed prior to product implementation.
- Whether credit administration has an appropriate role in the development process, to effectively promote sound underwriting.
- That controls are in place to ensure that compliance and underwriting issues are incorporated into all new products.
- Ensure that the review and approval process includes all necessary participants involved in product development, prior to implementation.
- Whether the planning process requires MIS which is adequate for product supervision and administration and that it is operative prior to product implementation.

Credit Administration

1.   Determine Credit Administration's role in formulating policy, monitoring compliance to policy, and monitoring lending practices and portfolio quality.

Underwriting

1.   Evaluate management's process for ensuring that new loan quality is consistent with policy and the board's capacity and tolerance for risk by considering any significant changes in credit criteria and terms.

2.   Evaluate the credit scoring systems, or other criteria, used for credit underwriting. If scoring systems are used, determine the following:

- How they were developed?
- If they are monitored and periodically revalidated?
- If they effectively rank order risk?
- How the cutoff scores and decision criteria were established?
- How does the portfolio distribution by credit score as of the examination date compare to prior periods.

3.   If the bank engages in preapproved lending, determine if the programs have been adequately "tested" prior to any large-scale credit offering.

4.   Evaluate the adequacy of the process management uses to monitor new loan volume.

5.   Determine whether the bank incorporates and enforces prepayment penalties on

its loans.

6. Determine whether the bank periodically assesses how a substantial increase in interest rates may affect the credit performance of its residential, home equity, reverse mortgage, and affordable housing portfolios.

Loans and Participations Purchased and Sold

1. Evaluate management's process for exercising controls and procedures over loans serviced for others (should be similar to those exercised for loans in the bank's own portfolio).

Collections

1. If automated collection systems are used, assess the systems' strengths and limitations by:

   - Determining whether systems interface with each other.
   - Reviewing key MIS reports produced by each system.

2. Review management's collection strategies. Consider:

   - How strategies are established.
   - How management measures the effectiveness of their strategies.

Asset Securitization

1. Evaluate management's planning process for ensuring adequate systems are in place to service current and anticipated securitizations.

Home Equity Lines

1. Evaluate how management performs periodic reviews of home equity lines (particularly when the line has been inactive and/or is nearing maturity), to prevent a "crisis based" evaluation.

2. Evaluate how customers are prohibited from exceeding their maximum approved lines.

3. Ensure procedures are in effect to prompt a review of home equity credit lines when management becomes aware of a change in a borrowers financial status or creditworthiness. Procedures should include an evaluation of the following:

   - Credit bureau report.
   - New financial report.

- Payment history.
- Verification of employment.
- Revaluation of collateral.
- Verification of first mortgage balance.
- Reassessment of loan-to-value requirement.

4. If the bank has substantial volumes of home equity loans with unspecified maturities, determine the methods used to assess the effective maturities or repricing dates for those loans.

5. Determine that home equity lines are capped and converted into term loans, if the loan-to-value requirement is exceeded during the term of the line.

Loan Records

1. Determine whether adequate processes have been implemented to ensure the accuracy of loan records. Consider:

   - Is the preparation and posting of subsidiary records performed or adequately reviewed by persons who do not also:
     - Issue official checks and drafts singly?
     - Handle cash?
   - Are subsidiary records reconciled daily with the appropriate general ledger accounts and reconciling items investigated by persons who do not also handle cash?
   - Are loan officers prohibited from processing loan payments?
   - Are delinquent account collection requests and past-due notices:
     - Checked to trial balances used in reconciling subsidiary records to general ledger accounts?
     - Handled only by persons who do not also handle cash?
   - Are inquiries about line/loan balances received and investigated by persons who do not also handle cash?
   - Are documents supporting recorded credit adjustments checked or subsequently tested by persons who do not also handle cash (if so, explain briefly)?
   - Is a daily record maintained summarizing transaction details (i.e., loans made, payments received, and interest collected), to support applicable general ledger account entries?
   - Are frequent note and liability ledger trial balances prepared and reconciled to controlling accounts by employees who do not process or record loan transactions?
   - Are current appraisals written, dated, signed, and in the files?
   - Have state laws been adequately researched to ensure that lien priority status

is maintained?
- Are properties under foreclosure proceedings segregated?
- Is an overdue report generated frequently (if so, how often)?

Loan Interest and Fees

1. Determine if adequate processes have been implemented to ensure accurate transactions relating to loan interest and fees. Consider:

   - Is the preparation, addition and posting of interest and fee records performed or adequately reviewed by, and any review performed by, persons who do not also:
     - Issue official checks or drafts singly?
     - Handle cash?
   - Are any independent interest and fee computations made and compared or tested to initial interest and fees records by persons who do not also:
     - Issue official checks or drafts singly?
     - Handle cash?

Personnel

Conclusion: Management (does/does not) have the skills and knowledge necessary to manage the risk inherent in residential, home equity, reverse mortgage, and affordable housing lending.

Objective: To determine management's ability to conduct residential, home equity, reverse mortgage, and affordable housing lending in a safe and sound manner.

1. Evaluate department structure and management's experience by:

   - Reviewing the organizational chart in conjunction with management's resumes.
   - Reviewing any management-prepared staffing analyses and determining if staffing levels are adequate considering present and future plans.
   - Ascertaining management's knowledge of current policies and procedures through discussions.

2. Determine significant current and previous work experience of management and significant lending personnel. Consider previous residential, home equity, reverse mortgage, and affordable housing:

   - Lending experience.
   - Administrative experience.

- Workout experience.

3. Assess the adequacy of staffing in the collections area. Consider:

    - Collector and supervisor experience levels.
    - Staff openings.
    - Ratio of accounts to collectors.
    - Ratio of collectors to supervisors.
    - Delinquency levels and trends.
    - Portfolio growth.

4. Assess management's technical knowledge and ability to manage residential, home equity, reverse mortgage and affordable housing lending based on the examination results of the quantity of risk and quality of risk management procedures.

Controls

Conclusion: Management and the board (have/have not) implemented effective control systems.

Objective: To determine the adequacy of loan review, internal/external audit, management information systems, and any other control systems as they relate to residential, home equity, reverse mortgage, and affordable housing lending.

1. Determine the effectiveness of the loan review system and/or audit function in identifying risk. Consider:

    - Scope and coverage of review(s). Is the following information addressed:
      - Credit quality?
      - Re-agings or extensions?
      - Override or override approvals?
      - Applicant credit scores?
      - Overlines?
      - Compliance with underwriting standards?
      - Compliance with policy?
      - Adequacy of internal controls?
      - Formalized annual home equity line reviews that include documentation to support the bank's use of a 50% risk weight for risk based capital purposes?
    - Frequency of reviews.

- Qualifications of loan review and audit personnel.
- Comprehensiveness and accuracy of findings.
- Adequacy and timeliness of follow up.

2. For the most recent loan review report of residential, home equity, reverse mortgage, and affordable housing lending, determine if management has appropriately addressed concerns and areas of unwarranted risk.

3. Determine that management has appropriately addressed deficiencies noted in the most recent loan review and audit reports.

4. If the bank engages in preapproved lending, review controls, including audits performed, to ensure that the preapproved offers are consistent with credit criteria.

5. Determine if management information systems (MIS) provide management and the board with sufficient information to monitor credit underwriting and the quality of the portfolio by:

- Reviewing reports used to monitor levels and trends in the following:
  - Renewals.
  - Extensions.
  - Overlimits.
  - Delinquencies.
  - Foreclosures.
  - Losses.
  - Recoveries.
  - Outdated appraisals.
  - Stagnant maximum usage balances.
  - Home equity lines with excessive usage in one day or one billing period.
  - Overrides by type/reason and officer.

6. Evaluate the MIS used to monitor type and quality of new loan volume. Consider:

- If reports track loan volume by product.
- If reports track exceptions to policy guidelines.

7. Evaluate the adequacy of securitization MIS at the board and management levels.

8. If credit scoring is used, determine if management uses credit scores to track the distribution of new loans by scores and to track the entire portfolio distribution as a method of managing risk. Do they also track delinquency distribution and override exception reasons?

9. If outside vendors are used for direct mail marketing efforts, ensure that the bank

regularly audits the vendor's controls and procedures.

10.   Determine if controls are in place to prohibit line advances to make scheduled payments.

11.   If the bank has substantial volumes of mortgage products and other loans with explicit caps, determine whether the bank monitors and evaluates the effect of those caps on the bank's future earnings and at what level of interest rates those caps would come into effect.

Conclusion

Objective: Determine overall conclusions and communicate examination findings regarding the quantity of risk, and management's ability to identify, measure, monitor, and control risk in residential, home equity, reverse mortgages and affordable housing lending operations.

Objective: Initiate corrective action when policies, practices, procedures, or control systems are deficient or when violations of law, rulings, or regulations have been noted.

1. Provide the EIC with a brief conclusion memo regarding:

   - Quantity of risk. Consider:
     - Credit quality and collectability of the portfolio, including trends in outstandings, delinquencies, and losses.
     - Compliance with established guidelines.
     - Compliance with applicable laws, rulings, and regulations.
   - Quality of risk management. Consider:
     - Adequacy of policies and underwriting standards.
     - Adequacy of processes, including planning.
     - Management's ability to conduct residential, home equity, reverse mortgage, and affordable housing lending in a safe and sound manner.
     - Adequacy of control systems, including loan review, audit, and management information systems.
   - Bank management's response to recommendations.
   - What the OCC needs to do in the future to effectively supervise residential, home equity, reverse mortgage, and affordable housing lending, including supervisory objectives, timing of activities, and staffing requirements.

2. Determine the impact on the aggregate and direction of risk assessments for any applicable risks identified by performing the above procedures. Examiners should refer to guidance provided under the OCC's large and community bank risk assessment programs.

   - Risk Categories: Compliance, Credit, Interest Rate, Liquidity, Reputation, Strategic, Transaction
   - Risk Conclusions: High, Moderate, or Low
   - Risk Direction: Increasing, Stable, or Decreasing

3. Determine, in consultation with EIC, if the risks identified are significant enough to

merit bringing them to the board's attention in the report of examination. If so, prepare items for inclusion under the heading Matters Requiring Board Attention.

- MRBA should cover practices that:
  - Deviate from sound fundamental principles and are likely to result in financial deterioration if not addressed.
  - Result in substantive noncompliance with laws.
- MRBA should discuss:
  - Causative factors contributing to the problem.
  - Consequences of inaction.
  - Management's commitment for corrective action.
  - The time frame and person(s) responsible for corrective action.

4. Discuss findings with management, including conclusions regarding applicable risks.

5. As appropriate, prepare a brief comment for inclusion in the report of examination.

6. Prepare a memorandum or update the work program with any information that will facilitate future examinations.

7. Update the OCC's Electronic Information System and any applicable report of examination schedules or tables.

8. Organize and reference working papers in accordance with OCC guidance.